Growing in Christian Discipleship

Evangelism Study Series

Volume 4

Joel D. Kline

faithQuest
the trade imprint of Brethren Press
Elgin, Illinois

Growing in Christian Discipleship
Evangelism Study Series, Volume 4
Joel D. Kline

Copyright © 1993 by *faithQuest*, the trade imprint of Brethren Press, 1451 Dundee Avenue, Elgin, Illinois 60120

All rights reserved. No portion of this book may be reproduced in any form or by any process or technique without the written consent of the publisher, except for brief quotations embodied in critical articles or reviews.

Biblical quotations, unless otherwise noted, are from the New Revised Standard Version of the Bible, copyrighted 1989 by the Division of Christian Education, National Council of Churches, and are used by permission.

Cover design by Jeane Healy

97 96 95 94 93   4 3 2 1

Library of Congress Cataloging-in-Publication Data

Kline, Joel D.
    Growing in Christian Discipleship / Joel D. Kline.
      p. cm. (Evangelism study series; v. 4)
      Includes bibliographical references.
      ISBN 0-87178-328-2 (pbk.) : $4.95
        1. Disciplining (Christianity) 2. Christian life – Brethren authors.
    I. Title. II. Series
    BV4520.K555   1993
    248.4'865–dc20   92-18484
                                                                                        CIP

Manufactured in the United States of America

Contents

Purpose of the Study 4
Introduction 5
Suggestions for Participants and Leaders 6
1. God and God Alone 11
2. The Importance of the Word 21
3. When You Pray 31
4. Praise to the Lord... 41
5. Walking by the Spirit 53
6. 'Tis a Gift to Be Simple 63
7. A Faith That Works....................................... 73
8. More Than Conquerors! 83
Endnotes... 91

Purpose of the Study

1. To explore scriptures that provide insights and models for helping people to grow in Christian discipleship
2. To discern learnings that call for personal action
3. To respond to those calls
4. To support others in their commitments to study and action

Introduction

"Go therefore and make disciples of all nations, baptizing them in the name of the Father and of the Son and of the Holy Spirit and teaching them to obey everything that I have commanded you. And remember, I am with you always, to the end of the age" (Matt. 28:19-20).

This is the Great Commission. Traditionally people have put the emphasis in these verses on the verb *go*. To be faithful to this commission, many have said, is to venture forth, going into all the world to reach people.

But a closer reading of this text emphasizes yet another part of the verse. A literal rendering of Matthew 28:19-20 from the New Testament Greek underscores the phrase "make disciples."

Faithful evangelism and church growth then are not just a matter of going, or even of baptizing. They also require discipling. As Philip Teng has observed, "The real strength of a church is not in the number of baptized members but rather in the number of disciples."[1] In the chapters that follow, we will discover what it means to be a Christian disciple. Both inward and outward journeys of faith will be explored as we find discipleship touching all of life.

This material expands on the four keys for growing in Christian discipleship: (1) *experiencing the power of the Spirit;* (2) *grounding oneself in God's word;* (3) *changing one's lifestyle;* (4) *committing oneself to service and prophetic witness.*

The need for followers of Christ has never been greater, people committed to Jesus as both Savior and Lord. Read on then and enroll in the school of discipleship. Sense the presence of the master teacher and discover again, or for the first time, the Christian way.

Suggestions for Participants and Leaders

For All Group Members

1. Pray daily for yourself and other group members to
    a. become increasingly aware of God's presence and power;
    b. discern God's messages presented in the scriptures;
    c. recognize and use opportunities for communicating the gospel.
2. Prepare thoroughly for each session by
    a. beginning well in advance;
    b. using the PREPARATION FOR THE NEXT SESSION sections in the book as a guide;
    c. reading the scripture text;
    d. writing your first responses to the passage in the space provided;
    e. reading the chapter;
    f. using the REFLECTING ON THE SCRIPTURES questions to pause in your reading and allow yourself some time to meditate just on the scripture for five to ten minutes;
    g. using the RESPONDING TO THE SCRIPTURES to contemplate how the scripture touches your life and how you might change in light of your learnings;

  h. marking phrases and writing questions and comments in the margin in order to remember and reinforce what you are learning.

3. Be a helpful group member by
   a. attending all sessions;
   b. practicing good listening skills;
   c. enabling others to feel included, valued, and secure in sharing;
   d. supporting other group members in their efforts to discern and respond to God's call for their lives.

4. If you are using a paraphrased or amplified version such as *The Living Bible*, be sure you also read the scripture texts in a standard translation such as the New Revised Standard Version or the New International Version.

5. Be aware that this study is typical of most areas of life. You will "reap what you sow." You will receive from it in proportion to what you give to it.

6. Be aware also that this study calls for action responses to learnings. In addition to studying this book and participating in discussion sessions, you will be applying what you learn to your daily life.

For Leaders

1. In preparation for your leadership role, complete the sentences in REFLECTING ON THE SCRIPTURES and RESPONDING TO THE SCRIPTURES found in each chapter. Mark the sentences in RESPONDING TO THE SCRIPTURES that you feel would be most helpful to the group.

2. Be prepared to share your thoughts and feelings as a way to encourage group involvement.

3. Begin and end sessions promptly.

4. During each session
   a. Begin with prayer for openness to the mind of Christ and the leading of the Spirit.
   b. Read the scripture text aloud.
   c. Discuss initial responses to the scripture.
   d. Discuss the questions in REFLECTING ON THE SCRIPTURE.
   e. Discuss the sentences in RESPONDING TO THE SCRIPTURE.
   f. Invite additional comments.
   g. Review the PREPARATION FOR THE NEXT SESSION.
   h. Close with an appropriate song, prayer, or affirmation of faith.

5. Guide the discussions of RESPONDING TO THE SCRIPTURES toward specific, appropriate, individual responses so that time is not spent on generalities that lead to little or no action.

6. Monitor the time carefully to allow for discussion of at least all of the questions you decided would be most helpful.

7. Involve participants by inviting them ahead of time to lead in prayer, to dramatize the scripture, to prepare an appropriate closing, etc.

8. Allow for all points of view to be expressed by group members. It is not essential that everyone speak, but it is important that no one or two person(s) dominate the discussion and that everyone knows that they have the right to speak.

9. At the end of Session 4, ask participants to prepare for Session 5 by completing RESPONDING TO THE CALL FOR ACTION as well as the usual PREPARATION FOR THE NEXT SESSION.

10. Begin Session 5 with a brief sharing of what the participants have written in response to items 1 through 4 in

RESPONDING TO THE CALL FOR ACTION. Divide into small groups of three or four people each and allow about ten minutes for this sharing. Watch the time carefully.

11. Begin Sessions 6, 7, and 8 with a time of sharing as a total group or in twos or threes. Ask how participants are doing with their RESPONSES TO THE CALL FOR ACTION. Encourage participants to support one another in their efforts. Allow about ten minutes for this and watch the time carefully.

12. Allow time at the end of Session 8 for completing and sharing the responses to RESPONDING TO THE CALL FOR ACTION.

13. Evaluate the past session prior to planning for the coming one.

1

God and God Alone

Purpose

- To acknowledge that Christian discipleship is rooted in a radical loyalty to God

Reading the Scriptures

Read Exodus 20:1-3 and Luke 4:5-8.
My first responses to these passages are...

Exploring the Scriptures

Exodus 20:1-3

In the Old Testament the Book of Exodus plays a role comparable to that of the four Gospels in the New Testament.[1] The Gospels are based upon the events of Christ's life, ministry, death, and resurrection, and yet they are much more than a historical record of those events. The Gospels are written from the perspective of faith, penned so that "you may believe that Jesus is the Christ, the Son of God, and that by believing you may have life in his name" (John 20:31 NIV).

In similar fashion the Book of Exodus is rooted in historical event, God's deliverance of the Hebrew people from bondage in Egypt. And yet, like the Gospels, Exodus is a book of faith. It moves beyond mere recounting of God's activity in freeing the Hebrews to an exploration of the meaning of that mighty deliverance, which results in the establishment of those Hebrews as a people, as a community of faith.

Actually, less than half of the Book of Exodus deals with Israel's departure from Egypt, while the larger part focuses on the aftermath of the Exodus, the institution and ordering of Israel's common life.[2] The Decalogue, more commonly known as the Ten Commandments and found in Exodus 20:1-17, plays a primary role in defining the people's relationship with God and with the community they form as God's chosen people. B. Davie Napier asserts that the Decalogue, also found in Deuteronomy 5:6-21 in a form differing only in a few details, represents "the summation of the will of the Lord for the community of Israel, drawn from an established body of legal and instructional material."[3] In other words, the Ten Commandments are the essence of God's message, God's word, to the people of Israel. The Commandments form the definition *par excellence* of the nature and shape of life rooted in relationship with God.

The Decalogue begins with the conviction that it is God who takes the initiative in relating and communicating with the people. "Then God spoke all these words: 'I am the LORD your God, who brought you out of the land of Egypt, out of the house of slavery' " (Exod. 20:1-2). At the core of that communication is the description of who God is and how God acts. God proclaims, "It was I who brought you from the closed to the open, from the bitter to the sweet, from the shackled to the free, from the lost to the saved!"[4] And that proclamation implies invitation as well, an invitation to know God, to acknowledge God, to identify with God. To truly know and to be intimately connected with God requires a response. As God is holy, so we are called to be holy, to respond to God's gracious love in joyful commitment and discipleship. God grants us freedom, and in freedom we respond to God's subsequent call for righteousness and worship.[5]

Immediately following God's self-identification as Deliverer comes the first of the commandments, "You shall have no other gods before me" (Exod. 20:3). Thus, the first and most fundamental summons is to absolute loyalty in worship and service. Even though the ancient Israelites are surrounded by people who worship other gods, the Lord does not condone worship of these competing deities. "No one can serve two masters" (Matt. 6:24), Jesus later proclaims, echoing God's demand for unswerving faithfulness. It is a sentiment reinforced by the second commandment, found in the verses that follow.

> You shall not make for yourself an idol, whether in the form of anything that is in heaven above, or that is on the earth beneath, or that is in the water under the earth. You shall not bow down to them or worship them; for I the LORD your God am a jealous God . . . (Exod. 20:4-5).

People of faith are to worship and serve God and God alone.

Luke 4:5-8

"In the last analysis there are only two things to worship– the true power and the false power; God or devil; God or self," asserts Joy Davidman in her book *Smoke on the Mountain: An Interpretation of the Ten Commandments.*[6] It is a choice Jesus faces when, following his baptism, he is led by the Spirit for forty days in the wilderness (Luke 4:1-2). Jesus stands ready to embark upon a ministry of proclaiming the kingdom of God and withdraws to determine strategy and methodology. What will be the shape of his ministry? To whom will he relate? How will he influence the society around him?

In the midst of Jesus' reflection, the tempter plants in his mind an image of a mountain from which the whole civilized world can be seen and offers, "If you, then, will worship me, it will all be yours" (v. 7). It is the temptation to seek first personal glory and power, not God's glory. Jesus, however, recognizes the danger of divided loyalty and cries out with determination, quoting from Deuteronomy 6, "It is written, 'Worship the LORD your God, and serve only him' " (Luke 4:8).

Reflecting on the Scriptures

1. Why is the first commandment so important as to be the first and not the second or the tenth, for example?

2. Why did Jesus choose to quote Deuteronomy 6:13 in response to the devil's temptation to control the world?

3. What does it mean about God, that God in Christ would refuse the power to control the world?

4. What other passages of scripture do these verses bring to mind?

Applying the Scriptures

An Inexorable Demand

In his book *Sermon on the Mount*, Clarence Jordan refers to the words of Jesus: "No one can serve two masters." Jordan writes:

> Notice that he doesn't say that you *shouldn't* serve two masters, but that you *can't*. This is not advice— it is law, as inexorable as the law of gravity. It's like stating that you can't follow a road that forks. It is based on the assumption that the mind of God and the mind of the secular world are in direct contradiction to each other. They give two conflicting standards of measurement. Loyalty must be given to one or the other.[7]

A Radical Demand

There is no middle ground in the Christian life. God demands our heart and soul and mind; God demands our whole being. Indeed, God's demand is so primary that our relationship with God takes precedence even over our relationships with other people, even over ministry to the broken and the hurting. Writing in *The Living Reminder*, Henri Nouwen asserts:

> Over the years we have developed the idea that being present to people in all their needs is our greatest and primary vocation. The Bible does not seem to support this. Jesus' primary concern was to be obedient to his Father, to live constantly in his presence. Only then did it become clear to him what his task was in his relationships with people.... Perhaps we must continually remind ourselves that the first commandment

requiring us to love God with all our heart, all our soul, and all our mind is indeed the first. I wonder if we really believe this. It seems that in fact we live as if we should give as much of our heart, soul, and mind as possible to our fellow human beings, while trying hard not to forget God. At least we feel that our attention should be divided evenly between God and our neighbor. But Jesus' claim is much more radical. He asks for a single-minded commitment to God and God alone.[8]

How seriously do we heed this call to singleminded commitment to the living God? Are we willing to go beyond a once-and-done commitment, continually surrendering to this God who demands our all? Do we see our commitment to love God as so primary in our lives that our relationship with God gives shape and direction to all our other relationships and responsibilities?

A Joyful Demand

There are some who are tempted to portray such thoroughgoing commitment to God as a dull and joyless drudgery. But the motivation for our discipleship is not obligation; it is gratitude that ours is a God who delivers us from bondage, who sets us free to experience the gift of life abundant and eternal. We respond joyously to the call to "worship the Lord your God and serve only him" (Luke 4:8 TEV), convinced that God and God alone is worthy of our ultimate loyalty. Writing in *The Cost of Discipleship*, German pastor and theologian Dietrich Bonhoeffer questions,

> And if we answer the call to discipleship, where will it lead us? What decisions and partings will it demand? To answer this question we shall have to go to him, for only he knows the answer. Only Jesus

Christ, who bids us follow him, knows the journey's end. But we do know that it will be a road of boundless mercy. Discipleship means joy.[9]

Responding to the Scriptures

1. Times when God has "taken the initiative" in relating and communicating with me have included . . .

2. God has freed me from the bondage of . . .

   and has given me the freedom to . . .

3. It is easiest to give God first place in my life when . . .

4. Situations in which I am tempted to compromise my loyalty to God are . . .

5. What gives those temptations power over me is . . .

6. A time away like Jesus' forty days in the wilderness would help me in my ministry of proclaiming the kingdom of God because . . .

7. If I were explaining to a new Christian the impossibility of serving two masters, I would say . . .

8. My commitment to God deepens my ministry to people when . . .

9. Experiences of worshiping God that have brought me joy are . . .

10. (To be completed following group discussion) My learnings from this session are . . .

Preparation for the Next Session

1. Pray daily for yourself and the other participants.

2. Share some of your "joy in faithfulness" with at least one person outside a faith community.

3. Read and consider the scripture text and content in Chapter 2.

4. Complete REFLECTING ON THE SCRIPTURES and RESPONDING TO THE SCRIPTURES in Chapter 2.

2

The Importance of the Word

Purpose
- To recognize the key foundational role of Scripture in undergirding Christian life and witness

Reading the Scriptures
Read 2 Timothy 3:10-17.
My first responses to this passage are...

Exploring the Scriptures
The two letters to Timothy and the letter to Titus share similar content and character and, therefore, are frequently studied as a unit. Commonly referred to as the pastorals, these three letters are unique among the letters of the Apostle Paul. They are addressed to individuals,

while the remaining Pauline letters, with the exception of the letter to Philemon, are written to churches. As a result, the pastorals have a distinctively personal flavor. At the same time, the three letters tell us a great deal about the developing organization of the early church, detailing qualifications for elders, bishops, and deacons. Indeed, some biblical scholars claim that the pastoral epistles depict a structure far too elaborate for the days in which Paul lived and ministered. Therefore, they doubt direct authorship by Paul. Instead, such scholars assume that a disciple of Paul must have written the letters in the Apostle's name, responding to particular concerns in the growing church as he believed Paul would respond. Yet the letters clearly do reflect an intimate relationship with the recipients, Timothy and Titus. Could it be that the letters were written by Paul but expanded and elaborated upon some years later by a church leader desiring to apply Paul's insights to a maturing and developing church? Asserts William Barclay,

> In the pastoral epistles we are still hearing the voice of Paul, and often hearing it with a unique personal intimacy; but we think that the form of the letters is due to a Christian teacher who summoned the help of Paul when the Church of the day needed the guidance which only he could give.[1]

Our passage from 2 Timothy 3:10-17 offers such guidance to a church troubled by false teachers, "holding to the outward form of godliness but denying its power" (3:5). Paul is urging Timothy to stand firm in the power of the Christian faith. "But as for you, continue in what you have learned and firmly believed . . . " (v. 14). It's a theme found not just in the third chapter, but throughout 2 Timothy. "Hold to the standard of sound teaching that you have heard from me, in the faith and love that are in Christ Jesus," writes Paul in the first chapter; then he continues, "Guard the good treasure entrusted to you, with the help of the Holy Spirit living in us" (1:13-14). A similar admonition is found in the final chapter of 2 Timothy. Paul warns Timothy that

The Importance of the Word

"the time is coming when people will not put up with sound doctrine, but having itching ears, they will accumulate for themselves teachers to suit their own desires" (4:3). Paul goes on to counsel Timothy: "As for you, always be sober, endure suffering, do the work of an evangelist, carry out your ministry fully" (4:5).

So that Timothy, whom the Apostle calls "my beloved child"(1:2), might remain faithful to his calling as a minister of Christ's gospel, the Apostle offers two resources. The first is Paul's own personal example: "Now you have observed my teaching, my conduct, my aim in life, my faith, my patience, my love, my steadfastness, my persecutions, and my suffering . . . " (3:10-11). Paul here is not speaking egotistically, but rather in the same vein as his admonition to the Corinthian Christians, "Be imitators of me, as I am of Christ" (1 Cor. 11:1). Because Paul's identity is so deeply rooted in Christ and Christ's ministry, Timothy will see Christ when he recalls the example of Paul. Paul so identifies with Christ that he willingly experiences persecutions and sufferings in the course of his ministry. "Indeed, all who want to live a godly life in Christ Jesus will be persecuted" (2 Tim. 3:12), Paul asserts. Life in Christ carries with it no guarantee of smooth sailing, no promise of a trouble-free life. And yet, life in Christ does carry the assurance that Christ's grace will surround us even in the midst of difficulty, just as the Lord rescued Paul from all persecutions (v. 11).

The second resource to which Paul points is the Scriptures. Paul urges Timothy to recall "how from childhood you have known the sacred writings that are able to instruct you for salvation through faith in Christ Jesus" (v. 15).

Scripture does not point to itself, "to faith in a Book, but to faith in the Person to whom the Book points. We are saved through faith in Jesus Christ."[2] This insight, of course, is given to us by Jesus himself, "It is they [the scriptures] which testify to me [Jesus]" (John 5:39). It is Christ himself, the one through whom God has spoken in such a complete and decisive way, who enables us to understand the message of the Scriptures.

All Scripture, states Paul, is "inspired by God" (2 Tim. 3:16). The biblical writers, as well as those whose witness contributed to their writing, were guided and empowered by God's Spirit. As a result, we are able to receive and to hear Scripture as God's own word addressed to us. Scripture is "useful for teaching, for reproof, for correction, and for training in righteousness," that we who love and serve God "may be proficient, equipped for every good work" (vv. 16, 17).

Paul's words underscore the crucial role the Scriptures play in the Christian community. To say that scripture is useful for teaching suggests that scripture shows us what we ought to believe. On the other hand, when Paul declares that scripture is useful for reproof, he means that through the Bible we learn what we ought not believe. When he says that scripture is useful for correction, he is telling us that the Bible teaches us how we ought not behave. And when he asserts that scripture provides training in righteousness, he is saying that the Bible tells us how we ought to behave. In short, writes Vernon Grounds in *Radical Commitment*, "Scripture teaches us *what to believe, what not to believe, how not to behave, how to behave.* We're further encouraged by this book to expect that as we behave righteously because of our right belief, we will become more and more like Jesus Christ."[3] We will be made "proficient, equipped for every good work."

Reflecting on the Scriptures

1. What are the "sacred writings" to which Paul refers in verse 15? How do we know?

2. How important for Timothy's learning is the example of others, including Paul?

3. Is it true that "*all* who *want* to live a godly life in Christ Jesus will be persecuted"?

4. What other passages of scripture does this passage bring to mind?

Applying the Scriptures

Yes, But How?

Vernon Grounds tells the story of a booklover who lends a prized volume to one of his friends. As that friend reads the book, he is puzzled. He notes that the initials YBH are frequently written in the margins, followed by a question mark. "What is the meaning of that symbol you've jotted down in the margin on so many pages, YBH?" the friend asks when he returns the book. "Oh, that means 'Yes, but how?' I am reading along, and I agree with what the author writes, only I wonder about making his ideas work in life. 'Yes. But how?'"[4]

It's a critical question to ask as we read and consider the Scriptures. How is it that scripture comes alive for us, moving us beyond the printed page to an encounter with the Living Word, with Jesus Christ? For surely that's the fundamental intent of the Scriptures. Walter Brueggemann suggests that "scripture reading can provide us with resources and images enabling us to understand, embrace and respond to life in all its richness. For the Bible presents human life in terms of the vitality of being in history with a covenantal partner [God in Christ] who speaks newness in a world which always seems fatigued and exhausted."[5] In other words, Brueggemann suggests that the central message of the Scripture is so powerful and so true that by itself it moves us to faith.

This can also be seen as the work of the Holy Spirit. The New Testament emerged from the early church's growing recognition of the need to give spiritual guidance and help to believers, as well as to encourage others to affirm Jesus as the Christ. Just as we believe that the Holy Spirit inspired those early writers, so we believe the same Spirit of God will provide us spiritual insight and understanding, enabling us to grasp God's message. A tract from colonial days in America suggests that

> Holy Scripture is a letter from God which he, through the working of his eternal Spirit, has caused to be written to the human race....
> Therefore it is urgently required of Christendom that all the words of Christ and his Spirit come to be so read, considered, and believed that they be carried with groanings in prayer to God; that they be received and appropriated in true contrition of heart; that the whole New Testament be written by the finger of God on the heart of the reader until his entire life becomes a living letter from God in which all men can read the commands of Christ (2 Cor. 3:3). It is not enough for a person to see the New Testament as a book where, indeed, the truth stands written, yet, nevertheless, one which does not greatly apply to us or does not commit us to the practice of the commands of Christ.[6]

Living Letters from God

There's an old adage for Christians that goes, "You may be the only Bible many people ever read." But we will be little prepared as living letters from God unless we discipline ourselves to study the Scriptures regularly and prayerfully. Spiritual leader Anna Mow, writing in her book *Say "Yes" to Life!*, contends, "We must eat the Word so that we may be nourished in our given relationship with our Living Lord and so that we may grow in that relationship."[7]

Rule of Faith and Practice

In order to grow in Christian discipleship, we must not only read the words of scripture, but allow the message to touch our spirit and infuse our very being. We are called to approach the Scriptures prayerfully, seeking to discern the mind of Christ for our daily lives and relationships. It is a matter of coming before the Word asking, What is God saying to me and about me through this passage of scripture? What would God have me do in faithful response to the message?

Scripture reading is not an end in itself; its goal is to lead us to the transforming Christ. Surely that's why James asserts in his letter, "Be doers of the word, and not merely hearers who deceive themselves" (1:22). J. B. Phillips' translation of the verse is perhaps more pointed: "Don't only hear the message, but put it into practice; otherwise you are merely deluding yourselves."

Tom Sine tells the story of a young couple recently committed to Christ, serious about putting the tough teachings of Christ into practice. Several years earlier Jan had undergone oral surgery and the surgeon, in the course of his work, had broken Jan's jaw. When the surgeon refused to compensate her for the obvious blunder, Jan and her husband, Jeff, filed suit to reclaim damages and lawyer fees. The case dragged on for three years. Then, two weeks before the insurance company was to send a settlement, Jan and Jeff changed their minds. For they had begun to ask themselves, "How can we follow Jesus' teachings to love this doctor and forgive him for breaking Jan's jaw, and still take him to court?" Said Jan, "The revolutionary love of Jesus makes it totally impossible for us to do anything but love him and forgive him." And so Jan and Jeff dropped the case, even though to do so created considerable financial hardship for them.[8]

Jan and Jeff not only heard the message of Christ; they sought to put it into practice. By their actions, they were attempting to give obedience to the words of Jesus. As much as they did this, their actions affirm with Paul that "all scripture is inspired by God and profitable for teaching, for reproof, for correction, and for training in righteousness." Genuine encounter with scripture leads us to become more and more like Jesus Christ, equipped for every good work.

Responding to the Scriptures

1. Some of my experiences with scripture are memorable because...

2. My appreciation of and love for God's word increases as I...

3. Scripture passages or concepts that are helpful in instructing me in how I ought to behave are ones that...

4. Scripture passages that most firmly root my identity in Christ and Christ's ministry are ones that...

5. Scripture passages that complete and equip me for good works are ones that . . .

6. If my life were a living letter from God, the "commands of Christ" that people would read in me are . . .

7. What most helps me be nourished by God's word is . . .

8. Barriers that hinder my putting into practice what I have learned from scripture are . . .

9. I can help new Christians develop appreciation and love for God's word by . . .

10. (To be completed following discussion) My learnings from this session are . . .

Preparation for the Next Session

1. Pray daily for yourself and the other participants.

2. Share with at least one other person how knowledge of the Scriptures has enriched your life.

3. Read and consider the scripture text and content in Chapter 3.

4. Complete REFLECTING ON THE SCRIPTURES and RESPONDING TO THE SCRIPTURES in Chapter 3.

3

When You Pray

Purpose

- To lift up the central role of prayer in growth as Christian disciples

Reading the Scriptures

Read Matthew 6:5-15.
My first responses to this passage are . . .

Exploring the Scriptures

The Sermon on the Mount, found in chapters five through seven of Matthew's Gospel, stands as the most extensive single collection of Jesus' teachings in any of the four Gospels. Many biblical scholars contend that the Sermon on the Mount isn't really a sermon at all, but rather the Gospel writer's collection of significant sayings and teachings of Jesus concerning discipleship. Clarence Jordan suggests, alternatively, that "instead of being a collection of sayings, the Sermon is a condensation of a much longer discourse."[1] Whatever its origin, the Sermon on the Mount occupies a central position in the New Testament, providing a vivid portrayal of the way our Lord envisions life and relationships. The Sermon is a description of life in the kingdom of God.

The theme for our passage from Matthew 6:5-15 can be found only verses earlier in 6:1: "Beware of practicing your piety before others in order to be seen by them; for then you have no reward from your Father in heaven." That verse introduces a section in which Jesus challenges us to examine our motives. As we share with the poor (vv. 2-4), as we engage in prayer (vv. 5-15) and fasting (vv. 16-18), what is our primary concern? Is it our desire to bring honor and glory to God, or is our greater yearning to achieve status and acclaim in the eyes of our fellow human beings?

Jesus doesn't mince words, labeling as hypocrites those who worship and serve only to gather applause from others. Why? Because public acts of piety can easily mask a selfish heart. An inner craving for recognition and acclaim can quickly become "a substitute for humble dependence on the power of God's Spirit alone."[2] Jesus offers several means for avoiding this hypocrisy.

> And then, when you pray, don't be like the play-actors. They love to stand and pray in the synagogues and at street corners so that people may see them at it. Believe me, they have had all the reward they are going to get. But when you pray, go into your own room, shut your door and pray to your Father privately (vv. 5-6 Phillips).

Jesus is concerned that his followers experience genuine connectedness with God, deep and abiding communion with God. Three times a day, 9:00 a.m., 12:00 noon, and 3:00 p.m., the faithful Jew of Jesus' day stops his work and turns toward Jerusalem to pray.[3] The hypocrite furtively arranges at prayer times to be at the center of human activity, so that the act of prayer can be seen and admired by others. Jesus, on the other hand, urges us to be alone with God, to enter into intimate conversation with God. It is not that Jesus opposes public and corporate prayer, for elsewhere he joins in worship in the synagogue. Further, the early Christians prayed together, forming a company "of one heart and soul" (Acts 4:32). But Jesus' words contain a stringent note of caution. Outward form is not enough; prayer must be a merging of the individual's spirit with the Spirit of God.

Jesus offers a second directive concerning prayer. "In your prayers do not babble as the pagans do, for they think that by using many words they will make themselves heard" (Matt. 6:7 JB). The Roman and Greek religions, which dominate the first-century Mediterranean world, are characterized by excessive words and ritual.[4] Their purpose? To cajole the gods into responding to the needs of the people. But our God, asserts Jesus, does not need to be coaxed into giving us what we need. Indeed, "your Father knows what you need before you ask him" (v. 8).

Jesus is not opposed to our petitioning God to meet particular needs, for on other occasions he teaches that we are to be persistent in prayer (see especially Luke 11:5-13, 18:1-8). But Jesus wants us to understand that prayer is far more than making one request after another. Prayer is trusting in God's care; prayer is listening for God's direction; prayer is yearning for the fullness of God to infuse our being.

With such an understanding of prayer in mind, Jesus shares a model prayer, traditionally labeled the Lord's Prayer. It might more accurately be named the "disciples' prayer," however, for it is a prayer given by Jesus to his followers. According to Luke, Jesus shares the prayer in response to a disciple's request, "Lord, teach us to pray" (Luke 11:1).

The prayer is brief, containing only 57 words in the original Greek, yet its influence on the world has been immeasurable. It has been on the lips of more people than any other piece of the world's greatest literature.[5] The Lord's Prayer "is personal, yet it is plural; it has a universal ring to it, and yet it honors human uniqueness and individuality."[6]

The Lord's Prayer takes us beyond self-centeredness, focusing our thoughts upon God and God's kingdom. The prayer begins by centering not on our troubles, problems, anxieties, and needs, but rather on the God who is addressed as "Our Father who art in heaven" (Matt. 6:9 KJV). Jesus makes frequent use of the title of "Father," suggesting that God is a living person, one with whom we may be intimately related. Even more, God is our Father, suggesting that we experience oneness not only with our Creator, but with the whole family of God.[7] We hold God's name, God's very nature, as "hallowed" or holy by participating in the unfolding of God's kingdom. And so the prayer continues, "Thy kingdom come. Thy will be done, on earth as it is in heaven"(v. 10 KJV).

What is the kingdom of God, but "the reigning activity of Christ over human hearts and society"?[8] To pray this petition, therefore, is to pray that God will "complete his great purpose of salvation begun in the life, death and resurrection of Jesus, the coming of the Spirit, the creation of the new Israel, which is the Church."[9] Further, it is to pray that we will personally invest our energies, our time, our resources in living and proclaiming God's kingdom and in doing God's will.

In order to participate in God's ministry and service, we need nourishment, both the physical nourishment of "daily bread" and the spiritual food of God's forgiveness. Maxie Dunnam asserts,

> Now comes the prayer for pardon: "And forgive us our debts as we also have forgiven our debtors." Notice the word *and*, linking the prayer for pardon with the request for bread. How clear the logic! Jesus knew that God offers two kinds of food: food for the body and food for the soul, one to sustain life, the other to make life free and whole.[10]

The petition for forgiveness is expanded after the prayer, in verses 14 and 15. Forgiveness is a two-way street. As we accept God's gift of forgiveness, we are freed to forgive others and to seek reconciliation in broken relationships. But if we maintain a bitter and unforgiving spirit toward others, we are refusing to allow God's forgiving grace to transform and empower us.

Jesus concludes the model prayer with a request of God, "And lead us not into temptation, but deliver us from evil" (v. 13 KJV). It is our honest acknowledgment that difficult times, times of testing, will surely come to us. Through it all, we need the power and strength of God's Spirit; we need the gift of divine guidance and protection. This final petition, therefore, expresses trust and confidence in God. Clarence Jordan writes, "For this is the prayer of the totally committed, the wholly surrendered, the completely dedicated citizens of the kingdom of God."[11]

Reflecting on the Scriptures

1. Why, do you suppose, does Jesus call God his "Father"?

2. Is prayer an individual event or a community event? What is your evidence from this particular scripture?

3. When we pray "Hallowed be thy name," are we asking that God would make his name hallowed or are we declaring that we are hallowing his name in our prayer?

4. What other passages of scripture does this passage bring to mind?

Applying the Scriptures

Lord, Teach Us to Pray

Prayer is a common experience among people of faith. Indeed, there is a sense that to pray is as natural as to eat and drink and breathe and sleep. We are likely to cry out to God in the face of difficulty or pain and to utter spontaneous expressions of gratitude when we encounter unexpected beauty or sudden good fortune. Apparently this tendency to pray is built into us. And yet a tendency to pray is quite different from an ongoing practice of prayer. After noting this human inclination toward prayer, former *Upper Room* editor Maxie Dunnam goes on to assert, "To live a life of prayer is something else. To pray consistently is not easy. It requires commitment and discipline. Don't condemn yourself if you find praying difficult. Most of us do."[12]

The problem is we frequently feel so alone in our struggles with prayer. Too often the church has communicated the message that Christians will automatically know how to develop a significant practice of prayer. As a result, when we find sustained prayer to be difficult, we are reluctant to confess our struggles to our fellow Christians. How crucial then that our congregations create an open and supportive climate in which questions and struggles, fears and doubts, can be faced honestly with the encouragement of brothers and sisters! And how crucial that you and I take the risk of verbalizing our need for growth in the art of prayer! Like the early disciples, we need to come individually and corporately before the Master, requesting "Lord, teach us to pray."

A Creative Rhythm

Anna Mow boldly attests that prayer is "the greatest adventure in the world. It is cooperating with God in the use of his power."[13] If we are to embark upon this great adventure, there can be no higher teacher than Christ Jesus himself. Scripture records that prayer was an integral part of our Lord's life. Christ not only commends prayer to his followers; he himself prays over and over again, testing his life by the standard of God's will and purposes. As a result, Christ's earthly ministry reflects a creative rhythm between times alone in prayer and times actively involved in outward expressions of ministry and obedient service. Our Lord's times in the "deserted place" (Mark 1:35) were not times of selfish withdrawal. Rather, they were crucial times for basking in God's presence and love, times for aligning himself afresh with God. Christ's times of solitude were times of praying, "Thy kingdom come. Thy will be done, on earth as it is in heaven."

No Longer Triflers

And so it is for us. To pray is to change. To pray is to allow God and God's kingdom to be central in our lives. To pray is to open ourselves to God's direction, God's guidance, God's vision for human life. Surely that's why the early Methodist leader John Wesley could say so emphatically,

> Whether you like it or no, read and pray daily. It is for your life; there is no other way; else you will be a trifler all your days. . . . Do justice to your soul; give it time and means to grow. Do not starve yourself any longer.[14]

When we resolve not to be triflers in life, but to open our hearts and minds intentionally to the transforming God in all situations, the distinction between prayer and action, between reflection and service, becomes blurred. Douglas V. Steere, in his book *Dimensions of Prayer*, illustrates this with the story of an overworked missionary nurse in a hospital in Angola. The nurse complained bitterly to her superior that, after her twelve hours on duty with many extra demands beyond her routine tasks, she simply was too worn out to pray. As a result, her interior life was withering away. Even when the nurse's long shift was supposed to be ending, she still had twelve patients to bathe. What did she have to look forward to, beyond collapsing in her room, exhausted beyond belief? The older colleague patiently listened to the outburst, then suggested it was not really necessary to wait until she got home to pray. If she would wash each of the twelve patients as though each were Christ, her praying would begin at once.[15] Life would be transformed.

To live and work and serve in a prayerful spirit radically alters our perspective. How might you and I make the familiar petition "Thy kingdom come. Thy will be done" come alive here and now in life's encounters and relationships?

Responding to the Scriptures

1. My earliest memories of prayer are ...

2. Prayers that I believe bring honor and glory to God are ones that ...

3. I feel in closest communion with God when ...

4. I am most likely to seek God's forgiveness when...

5. I am most likely to express forgiveness when...

6. My commitment to and discipline of prayer are...

7. In discipling a new believer I would illustrate the truth that prayer changes things by...

8. My prayers and actions are most closely aligned when...

9. I see the people I encounter as though they were Christ when...

10. (To be completed following discussion) My learnings from this session are . . .

Preparation for the Next Session

1. Pray daily for yourself and the other participants.
2. Continue evaluating your prayer life.
3. Read and consider the scripture text and content in Chapter 4.
4. Complete REFLECTING ON THE SCRIPTURES and RESPONDING TO THE SCRIPTURES in Chapter 4.

4

Praise to the Lord

Purpose
- To affirm the place of worship and praise in Christian discipleship

Reading the Scriptures
Read Psalm 100.
My first responses to these passages are...

Exploring the Scriptures

The Book of Psalms occupies a unique position among the biblical writings. As "the prayer book of the Bible," it reflects a deeply honest searching for intimate connectedness with the living God. While other portions of scripture focus far more on God's word addressed to humankind, the Psalms record personal reflections humans have directed to God. As a result, the Psalms display a myriad of emotions and moods, including joy and sorrow, fear and hope, rage and love. But the predominant mood communicated in the Book of Psalms is praise, celebrating who God is and how God acts in human life.

Not surprisingly, the Book of Psalms has played a significant role in Christian worship. Bernhard W. Anderson writes, "The early church was profoundly influenced by synagogue worship in which psalms were read as scripture, recited as prayers, and sung as hymns."[1] The Apostle Paul, writing to the Ephesians, urges his fellow Christians to "sing psalms and hymns and spiritual songs among yourselves, singing and making melody to the Lord in your hearts, giving thanks to God the Father at all times and for everything in the name of our Lord Jesus Christ" (Eph. 5:19-20). Similar instruction is found in the letter to the Colossians: "Let the word of Christ dwell in you richly; teach and admonish one another in all wisdom; and with gratitude in your hearts sing psalms, hymns, and spiritual songs to God" (Col. 3:16).

The 100th Psalm, though relatively brief (five verses), is a familiar one, which the church down through the centuries has appreciated for its forthright expression of praise and thanksgiving. Called by some "a psalm for the thank offering," it invites people of faith, not only in Israel but in "all the earth" (v. 1), to give thanks to God for his blessings. A procession of worshipers apparently stands ready to enter the gates and pass into the courts of the temple for a service of thanksgiving and thank offering. The procedure followed for presenting a thank offering to God is detailed in Leviticus 7:11-21, and Psalm 100 provides words of worship and praise to accompany the sharing of sacrificial gifts.

Psalm 100 is generally classified as a hymn, that category of psalms in which "the psalmist praises God in general terms, extolling him for who he is, for his majesty as Creator, and his mighty works in history."[2] In fact, the 100th Psalm actually consists of two short hymns (vv. 1-3, 4-5), each containing a call to worship and a statement describing the grounds for worship. This structure may well reflect the psalm's early use in worship, with the first hymn being sung by a choral group at the head of those processing to the temple gates, and the second hymn a response by another choir already within the temple, inviting the worshipers to enter the courts.[3]

The pilgrims who gather to worship are told: "Worship the Lord with gladness; come into his presence with singing!" (v. 2). Joy, here characterized by singing, is the distinguishing mark of all who would serve God. And the impetus for the gladness and joy of the worshiping congregation is their confidence in who and what God is. What follows in verse three and then in verse five provides a statement of faith for the people of Israel. This statement of faith includes six affirmations: (a) the Lord is God; (b) God is our Creator; (c) we are God's people; (d) the Lord is good; (e) God's steadfast love endures forever, and (f) God's faithfulness continues through all generations.[4]

The foundational point for the psalmist's worship and praise is knowledge of the Lord as God. To know God involves far more than mere acquaintance. Knowledge of God goes beyond intellectual acceptance of God's existence; it is a matter of experiencing firsthand the love and mercy and the presence and power of God. It is knowing that God our Creator claims us. Even more, God adopts us: "It is he that made us, and we are his; we are his people, and the sheep of his pasture" (v. 3). In other words, we are the special flock God chooses to shepherd. "By such a tender figure the character of the Lord's dominion over Israel is defined."[5] To confess faith in God as loving Creator of a people is to acknowledge absolute dependence on him. It is to attest that "the Lord is good" (v. 5), worthy of our trust. To affirm that "we are his" becomes by extension the confession that not only do I belong to God, but the whole earth is God's. Therefore, all creation is dependent on God for its being and meaning.[6]

When we are filled with assurance that God is trustworthy and gracious, our sense of thanksgiving and praise cannot be contained. The psalmist recognizes this and so invites those who have encountered God's goodness to respond with gratitude: "Enter his gates with thanksgiving, and his courts with praise. Give thanks to him, bless his name" (v. 4). As the people worship and praise, they remind themselves anew of God's character, a character of goodness and steadfast love and faithfulness that endures to all generations (v. 5).

Reflecting on the Scriptures

1. One of the purposes of the Psalms is to touch emotions. How does Psalm 100 touch your emotions?

2. Use your imagination to consider how the Israelites made "joyful noise"; served "the LORD with gladness"; came into the Presence with "singing"; and entered with "thanksgiving" and "praise."

3. How does your worship of God compare with the image you have for the people of Israel's worship?

4. What other passages of scripture does this passage bring to mind?

Applying the Scriptures

Good Work, God!

Presbyterian pastor John Killinger begins his book *The Cup and the Waterfall* by relating an event in the corridors of an airport crowded with people scurrying to and from their planes.

> Many were tired, and their faces reflected the tensions of a long day. Tempers were edgy as they hurried along, trying to make connections or get to taxicabs.
>
> Coming toward her in the crowd, my friend saw an elderly lady being pushed in a wheelchair by a younger companion. Suddenly, as they were almost abreast of one another, the elderly lady exclaimed, in a voice loud enough for everyone to hear, "Good work, God!"
>
> Nearly everyone in the corridor turned to look at the old lady and saw that she was looking out the windows of the corridor. Their eyes followed hers and saw a majestic sunset lighting up the sky.
>
> Smiles broke out on all the faces. Shoulders were squared and thrown back. Steps were lighter. The atmosphere of the entire place was transformed....[7]

There is something transforming about the experience of praising God. When we focus on the goodness and grace, the presence and strength of God in our lives, we are lifted beyond ourselves and our self-centeredness. We recognize that life's meaning is found, not as a result of our own efforts and strivings, but as a gift from God. And that's why worship is such a primary activity of the church. Worship reminds us that God invites us to be a part of something far greater than ourselves– the kingdom of God. And we are led into that kingdom through God's gift of Jesus Christ.

In his book *Worship Is a Verb*, Robert E. Webber asserts that

> The purpose of worship is not to prove the Christ it celebrates, but to bring the worshiper so in tune with God's reconciliation through Christ that his death and resurrection become a lived experience.... In Christian worship we are not merely asked to believe in Jesus Christ, but to live, die, and be resurrected again with him. Life is not an intellectual construct, but a journey of death and rebirth. When our life story is brought up into the story of Christ's life, death, and resurrection, it then gains meaning and purpose.[8]

Look Redeemed!

And yet we who take seriously the call to Christian discipleship and obedience stand in danger of losing sight of this element of celebration. It is easy to focus so intently on the duty of following Christ that we overlook the joy. Cruden, author of *Concordance of the Bible* published in 1769, wrote: "To laugh is to be merry in a sinful manner."[9] His statement is extreme, and yet today there are still those who view with suspicion any overt expression of joy or praise. Consequently, they approach worship as obligation, as duty, rather than as celebration.

The 19th-century skeptic Friedrich Nietzsche once said to a group of Christians of his day, "You are going to have to look more redeemed than you do if we are to believe the message of redemption."[10] Challenging words! They suggest that even those who are skeptical of the Christian faith recognize that its power is in its ability to transform and redeem human life. If we have encountered the renewing grace of God through Jesus Christ ought we not be joyfully worshiping and praising our God?

A Complete Triangle

When our worship fails to provide significant opportunity for praise, something critical is lacking. Von Hugel once observed, "Any religion that ignores the adoration of God is like a triangle with one side left out."[11] A triangle with only two sides is no triangle at all; so worship without praise is not worship at all.

The Book of Psalms is so significant in Christian worship because it helps complete the triangle. Again and again the psalmists pour out their hearts, expressing anger, hurt, confusion, and pain. Yet through it all there is an unceasing yearning for life intimately connected with God. And through it all the element of praise abounds. When the psalmists remind themselves of what God has done for them in the past, they are assuring themselves of God's continuing love and care.

Is this not the same in Christian worship? Worship is a time for recalling God's gracious gift of Jesus Christ. Worship is a time for affirming God's goodness, for crying out in our souls, "Good work, God!" Worship is a time for giving thanks to God. And worship is a time for acknowledging who we are and whose we are: "Know that the Lord is God! It is he that made us, and we are his; we are his people, and the sheep of his pasture" (Psa. 100:3).

How else are we to respond, but by entering God's presence with thanksgiving, singing praises, and serving God with gladness! For "praise is the basic and inevitable response to rediscovery of the activity of God, to the fresh awareness 'from whom all blessings flow.' "[12] Let us be a worshiping people, a people of praise.

Responding to the Scriptures

1. My spontaneous expressions of praise are often inspired by ...

2. I give thanks for everything when...

3. I hesitate to give thanks for all things when...

4. If a new Christian would ask me to explain my identity as a "chosen" child of God, I would say...

5. I first experienced dependence on God for meaning in my life when...

6. I acknowledge my absolute dependence on God by...

7. One of my transforming experiences of praise was...

8. A contemporary person who "looks redeemed" is . . .

9. Worship is celebration for me when . . .

10. (To be completed following discussion) My learnings from this session are . . .

Preparation for the Next Session

1. Pray daily for yourself and the other participants.

2. Read and consider the scripture text and content in Chapter 5.

3. Complete REFLECTING ON THE SCRIPTURES and RESPONDING TO THE SCRIPTURES in Chapter 5.

4. Complete RESPONDING TO THE CALL FOR ACTION (found on page 50).

Responding to the Call for Action

1. The new things I have learned that are calling me to grow in Christian discipleship are...

2. The actions to which they are calling me are...

3. The new things I have learned that are calling me to help disciple others are...

4. The actions to which they are calling me are...

5. During the next four weeks, I will seek to grow in discipleship and disciple others by...

I will ask _____ to help me be accountable for the above actions.

5

Walking by the Spirit

Purpose
- To emphasize the importance of "walking by the Spirit" in one's character and relationships

Reading the Scriptures
Read Galatians 5:13-25.
My first responses to this passage are . . .

Exploring the Scriptures
Paul's letter to the Galatians has frequently been labeled the Magna Charta of Christian liberty, the epistle of Christian freedom. It is a letter that "blazes with passion and must have come red-hot out of the writer's heart! It is not a treatise but a sword-cut in a battle, dealt in an hour of

great peril by a combatant facing formidable foes."[1] Paul's foes are Judaizers, a group of Jewish Christians convinced that gentile converts must first submit themselves to Jewish law, to circumcision, before embracing Christianity. Apparently a number of Judaizers have followed the Apostle Paul at the churches in Galatia and are intentionally undermining Paul's ministry. The Judaizers question Paul's qualifications as an apostle and contradict Paul's teaching that a person "is justified not by the works of the law but through faith in Jesus Christ" (Gal. 2:16).

Upon hearing that the same "foolish Galatians" (3:1) are "quickly deserting the one who called [them] in the grace of Christ" and are turning to some who "want to pervert the gospel of Christ" (1:6-7), Paul reels off an impassioned letter. The Apostle reiterates the message he proclaimed when he ministered among the Galatians– that salvation is a gift of God. It is not something we earn, but rather something we joyfully receive as a gracious gift. Paul reaches the apex of his writing in chapter five when he cries out, "For freedom Christ has set us free. Stand firm, therefore, and do not submit again to a yoke of slavery" (5:1).

Christians, Paul says, should be free to live in Christ, unhampered by a series of regulations and prohibitions. Yet Paul is not unaware that there is danger in his position, that there may be those who will twist and abuse this gospel of Christian freedom. Such people seek to make of their freedom in Christ a license to do whatever they selfishly desire. With such distortions of his message in mind, Paul pens the words that form the focus of this study. William Barclay translates Paul in 5:13-14:

> It was for freedom that you were called, only you must not use this freedom as a bridgehead through which the worst side of human nature can invade you, but in love you must serve one another; for the whole law stands complete in one word, in the

sentence, "You must love your neighbor as yourself."[2]

These verses signal a shift in the letter as Paul turns from theological discussion to practical advice. Paul now discusses how it is that disciples of Christ are to live out their freedom. For Paul freedom means servanthood, the willingness to seek the best for others, to follow the way of self-giving love in encounters and relationships. To support his contention, Paul quotes a familiar verse from Leviticus 19:18: "You shall love your neighbor as yourself." Jesus, too, uses that quotation when asked, "Which commandment is the first of all?" After responding, "The first is ... you shall love the Lord your God with all your heart, and with all your soul, and with all your mind, and with all your strength,' " Jesus continues, "The second is this, 'You shall love your neighbor as yourself' " (Mark 12:28-31).

But how is it that we live out this kind of servanthood, loving neighbor as self? Paul makes it clear that we do not do so on our own strength alone, but only through the power of God's Holy Spirit. Commentator William Neil writes, "Since the gift of the Spirit was given to the Church at Pentecost (Acts 2), there is a power available to help men and women who try to live their lives in accordance with the pattern set by Jesus, which they accept as God's will for themselves and the rest of the world."[3] Even as this power is available to us, we nevertheless experience an internal battle, "a steady and relentless tug of war" between what Paul labels the desires of the flesh and the desires of the Spirit.[4] By desires of the flesh, Paul means not just sexual desires, but "our unregenerate lower nature, with all its unlovely appetites and impulses– human nature as tainted by sin and apart from the grace of God."[5] To live by the flesh is to allow self-centeredness to reign supreme in our lives. Life in the flesh is life separated from God, and those who are not connected with God are likely to "bite and devour one another" (Gal. 5:15).

Life in the Spirit, on the other hand, is life intimately connected with God, life in which we allow our attitudes and actions, our values and behavior, to be guided by the Spirit. To demonstrate just how radically different life in the flesh is from life in the Spirit, Paul shares two contrasting lists. The works of the flesh which lead to the path of self-indulgence stand over against the fruit of the Spirit. The Jerusalem Bible offers the following translation of verses 19-21, describing life cut off from relationship with the living God:

> When self-indulgence is at work the results are obvious: fornication, gross indecency and sexual irresponsibility; idolatry and sorcery; feuds and wrangling, jealousy, bad temper and quarrels; disagreements, factions, envy; drunkenness, orgies and similar things. I warn you now, as I warned you before: those who behave like this will not inherit the kingdom of God.

In contrast, asserts Paul, God's Holy Spirit can produce within us a whole new character, a lifestyle that reflects the self-giving way of Jesus Christ. "What the Spirit brings is very different: love, joy, peace, patience, kindness, goodness, trustfulness, gentleness and self-control" (vv. 22-23 JB). Then Paul adds, "There can be no law against things like that, of course" (v. 23 JB), reiterating that such a quality of living "has nothing to do with striving to observe the terms of any set of rules. It comes from commitment to Christ and from that alone."[6]

Commitment to Jesus Christ involves dying to the old and rising to the new. "You cannot belong to Christ Jesus unless you crucify all self-indulgent passions and desires" (v. 24 JB), something we are able to do only as we surrender ourselves as completely as possible to Christ, relying upon Christ's Spirit to form within us new character and new life direction. For Paul this experience of dying and rising is the very pattern of the Christian life. "By committing ourselves to Christ, and by baptism," writes William Neil, "we die symbolically to our past life and rise again to a new life which Christ lives in us."[7] Then we are empowered to conquer self-indulgence and to put on the way of self-giving servanthood. "Since the Spirit is our life, let us be directed by the Spirit" (v. 25 JB).

Reflecting on the Scriptures

1. What is your evaluation of the two lists: works of the flesh and fruits of the Spirit? Do they seem correct and adequate?

2. The way of the law and the way of the Spirit are attempting to achieve the same goals. What seems to be the most important difference between the law and the Spirit as a way to salvation?

3. What other passages of scripture does this passage bring to mind?

Applying the Scriptures

Our Many Selves

Elizabeth O'Connor has written a book entitled *Our Many Selves* in which she shares that

> It was during a time of painful conflict that I first began to experience myself as more than one. It was as though I sat in the midst of many selves. Some urged me down one path and some another. Each presented a different claim and no self gave another self an opportunity to be fully heard.[8]

It is a classic statement of the kind of inner turmoil and confusion that results from conflict between what Paul labels as desires of the flesh and desires of the Spirit. We feel ourselves pulled in a host of directions, torn by competing loyalties until we find a center in Jesus Christ. The freedom Christ brings to us is not a matter of having no master or focus in our lives, but it is a freedom to accept a new Master, Christ Jesus the Lord. As we commit ourselves to Christ, we are set upon a journey toward wholeness; Christ can bring unity and integration to our many selves, redeeming us from self-indulgence. With our Lord's help we can choose to walk by the Spirit, allowing our goals and attitudes, our character and behavior, to be molded and transformed by that Spirit.

A Saving Nature

Our new nature in Christ is illustrated by a story that Henri Nouwen tells of an old man who meditated daily beside the Ganges River in India. One day the old man saw a scorpion trapped in the roots of a tree growing on the bank. The more it tried to get free, the more entangled it became. So the old man reached out to save the frantic spider, but each time he got close enough to touch it, the scorpion stung the old man. Still the old man kept trying:

> At that moment, a passer-by saw the old man stretched out on the roots struggling with the scorpion and shouted, "Hey, stupid old man. What's wrong with you? Only a fool risks his life for such an ugly, useless creature. Don't you know you may kill

yourself trying to save that ungrateful animal?" Slowly the old man turned his head, and, looking calmly in the stranger's eyes, he said, "Friend, just because it is the nature of the scorpion to sting, why should I give up my nature to save?"[9]

A Jesus Style of Relating

When we are in Christ, when we walk by the Spirit, life takes on a new quality. "For anyone who is in Christ, there is a new creation; the old creation has gone, and now the new one is here" (2 Cor. 5:17 JB). With Christ we take on a saving nature, we take on a serving nature. Even when the world around us would sting us again and again, Christ's Spirit empowers us to live by a different standard, the standard of self-giving love and servanthood. As Peter reminds his fellow Christians,

> For to this you have been called, because Christ also suffered for you, leaving you an example, so that you should follow in his steps. "He committed no sin, and no deceit was found in his mouth." When he was abused, he did not return abuse; when he suffered, he did not threaten; but he entrusted himself to the one who judges justly. He himself bore our sins in his body on the cross so that, free from sins, we might live for righteousness; by his wounds you have been healed. (1 Pet. 2:21-24)

We have been given an example to follow, and we have received the Spirit who enables us to die to sin, to the desires of the flesh, that we might live to righteousness, heeding the desires of the Spirit. When we do, we are drawn to Jesus' style of living and relating. To walk by the Spirit is to reflect our Lord's nature, serving, loving, reaching out to others, seeking God's best for them.

God's Spirit frees us to serve. "Only do not use your freedom as an opportunity for self-indulgence, but through love become slaves to one another" (Gal. 5:13).

Responding to the Scriptures

1. The idea that salvation is a gift rather than something to be earned became real to me when . . .

2. To someone new to Christianity, I would explain how freedom can be equated with servanthood by saying . . .

3. I am most aware of my need for the power of God's Holy Spirit when . . .

4. Some of my attitudes and values that have changed through the Spirit's guidance are . . .

5. A personal experience demonstrating the weakness of rules and regulations compared to the strength of being committed to Christ was . . .

6. I am torn by competing loyalties when . . .

7. Here are examples of ways that unity brings freedom:

8. A contemporary person who has the "nature to save" is . . .

9. I reflect our Lord's nature and seek the best for others when . . .

10. (To be completed following discussion) My learnings from this session are . . .

Preparation for the Next Session

1. Pray daily for yourself and the other participants.
2. Begin implementing your responses to the call for action.

3. Read and consider the scripture text and content in Chapter 6.

4. Complete REFLECTING ON THE SCRIPTURES and RESPONDING TO THE SCRIPTURES in Chapter 6.

6

'Tis a Gift To Be Simple

Purpose

- To discover Christ's call to a lifestyle of nonconformity and simplicity

Reading the Scriptures

Read Romans 12:1-2 and Matthew 6:25-33.
My first responses to these passages are . . .

Exploring the Scriptures

Romans 12:1-2

The Apostle Paul never finishes a letter "without coming down to brass tacks, so to speak, getting down to the particulars of living."[1] The Letter to the Romans is no exception, even though it is unique among Paul's writings.

For when writing this letter, Paul is communicating with a group of Christians with whom he has had no prior personal contact. As a result, the letter has a more formal tone and provides a more systematic record of Paul's faith convictions than is characteristic of letters to congregations Paul founded. Nevertheless, as in other Pauline letters, there is movement in Romans from the theological to the ethical, from a rehearsal of the gospel message to a consideration of the practical implications of living as Christ's people.

This shift to a description of the lifestyle that inevitably flows from faith in Jesus Christ is introduced in 12:1-2. Paul appeals to his fellow Christians "by the mercies of God." The motivation for the living of a faithful Christian life is gratitude. People of faith are grateful for God's mercies, God's gifts of wholeness and salvation through Christ. Because of their gratitude, the faithful present their "bodies as a living sacrifice" (v. 1).

Paul builds on familiar practice, for the offering of a sacrifice to God was central to ancient religion. But Paul asks for a sacrifice of a very different kind. Rather than presenting an animal or a cereal offering to God, people of faith present their very selves. It is not enough for Christians to offer their time, their talent, even their possessions to God; Christians offer their whole lives, all that they are, to God.

Such a sacrifice is a "continuously living action."[2] While former sacrifices involved the burning, the destruction, of the object offered to God, a living sacrifice presented by the Christian to God

> is not destruction, it is service; it is being-used. Old-time sacrifice was the offer of something less than oneself, to be removed from use. The new sacrifice required of Christians is nothing less than oneself, made fit for use, and used.[3]

Paul defines this presenting of ourselves before God, allowing God to work in us and through us, as our spiritual worship, our "true worship" (v. 1 TEV). In the very act of worshiping and serving God, we are transformed. "Do not be conformed to this world," cautions the Apostle, "but be transformed by the renewing of your minds" (v. 2). When we conform to the will and purposes of God, we may find ourselves at odds with the standards of the world. In Christ we accept new priorities, new values, new purpose; in short, we find a new center, a divine Center. No wonder Paul cries out on another occasion, "For anyone who is in Christ, there is a new creation" (2 Cor. 5:17 JB). Connected to Christ, we discover life in God's kingdom, and we hear the call to live as if God's kingdom of righteousness and peace, of mercy and grace, were fully here. We develop the ability "to discern the will of God, and to know what is good, acceptable, and perfect" (v. 2 NEB).

Here are the "brass tacks" Paul wants us to get down to: the call to offer our whole lives to God in faithful worship and service; to conform so to the will of God that we willingly stand over against those values and standards of the present age that are less than what God envisions for human life; to live now as if God's kingdom were fully here.

Matthew 6:25-33

Like Romans 12:1-2, the passage from Matthew 6:25-33 stresses the Gospel's call to live by new values and standards, by the norms and directives of God's kingdom. "But strive first for the kingdom of God and his righteousness" (Matt. 6:33), Jesus declares. "Be concerned above everything else with his Kingdom and with what he requires," reads the same command in Today's English Version. "To 'seek first,' " writes Lloyd Ogilvie, "is to urgently ask for and live as searching for God's will; to question our purpose, our reason for being, and our destiny."[4] In other words, all our desires, all our hopes, all our commitments, are to be understood in the light of our primary loyalty to Jesus Christ and to the kingdom Jesus opens before us.

It is from this conviction (that we are to put first things first) that the Master urges his followers to "put away anxious thoughts about food and drink to keep you alive, and clothes to cover your body. Surely life is more than food, the body more than clothes" (v. 25 NEB). John W. Miller asserts,

> Perhaps no teachings of Jesus strike a modern reader with more astonishment and perplexity than these. At first glance they seem to sound an almost idyllic note, as though meant for some far-off island untouched by the rush of modern life. What meaning can they have for us who must live in a technologically complex world and daily face economic problems undreamed of by those of an earlier generation?[5]

Do not Christ's words echo down through the centuries to us, to us who live in the world's most materialistic society, a society in which the more we have the more we seem to worry? When Jesus challenges us to "look at the birds of the air" and "consider the lilies of the field" (vv. 26, 28), is he not calling us to trust in the God who holds us to be "of more value" (v. 26) than the birds and the flowers? Could it be that we, just like those in the first century A.D., tend to live our lives in such anxious fretting about the trivia in life that we frequently overlook God's will for us in crucial relationships?[6]

In effect Jesus is asking of his followers: What is it that you hold as most important in life? Are you willing to let go of undue anxiety, of anxiety that keeps you from surrendering yourselves, heart and soul, to the living God? Are you ready to set your minds on God's kingdom, God's vision for life, before all else?

Reflecting on the Scriptures

1. Note the emphasis upon the *mind* in Paul's plea for renewal. Why would our minds be the first thing in our "spiritual" worship and "living sacrifice"? How does mind connect with the body?

2. It is said that conforming to the world is something one can do without changing his or her inner nature; but to be transformed is to be utterly changed at the core. Is this the change Paul is asking of disciples?

3. Does it make you anxious when you consider seeking "first his kingdom and his righteousness"? If so, does your anxiety come from lack of faith in God's ability and desire to provide your basic needs?

4. What other passages of scripture does this passage bring to mind?

Applying the Scriptures

Our Native Land

Noted missionary to India E. Stanley Jones once wrote:

> The most miserable people in the world are the people who are self-centered, who don't do anything for anybody, except themselves. They are centers of misery, with no exception. On the contrary, the happiest people are the people who deliberately take on themselves the sorrows and troubles of others. Their hearts sing with a strange wild

joy, automatically and with no exceptions. We are structured for the outgoingness of the love of the kingdom. It is our native land.[7]

When we seek first God's kingdom, when we measure our lives by the standard of our Lord's will and purposes, life is forever different. We find our native land. While the society around us encourages us to take care of ourselves, to look out for "number one," we discover the joy of living for Christ and for others. While our culture suggests that life's meaning is to be found in the accumulation of more and more possessions, we experience in Christ a peace and a purpose not dependent upon the size of our bank accounts or the make of our automobiles. Rather, our life's meaning stems from the quality of our relationships; it flows from a life centered in Jesus Christ.

Simple Gifts

It was a similar conviction that led the Shaker hymn writer to proclaim:

> 'Tis a gift to be simple.
> 'Tis a gift to be free.
> 'Tis a gift to come down where we ought to be
> And when we find ourselves in the place
>   just right
> 'Twill be in the valley of love and delight.
> When true simplicity is gained,
> To bow and to bend we shan't be ashamed.
> To turn, turn will be our delight.
> 'Till by turning, turning we come round
>   right.[8]

To live a life of simplicity is the result of "coming down where we ought to be," focusing our energies, prioritizing our commitments, discerning our callings in the light of Christ and Christ's kingdom. To live a life of simplicity is to discover the courage to go against the grain of the society around us, daring to be different because we have taken on new values and priorities through Jesus Christ.

The story of Bob and Janet Aldridge, a couple living with their ten children in California, demonstrates the difference a commitment to growing in Christian discipleship can make in our lives. Early on in their marriage, Janet and Bob decided that they would use their resources to raise good children and to do God's will as they discerned it for their lives. It was a decision of significant import, more than they realized at the time. For Bob soon came to be employed in the defense industry, an engineer helping design missiles. As the years in the 1960s and early 1970s passed, however, Janet and Bob became increasingly uncomfortable with the discrepancy between the faith they proclaimed and the source of their family income. The more seriously Bob and Janet took their faith, the more they struggled. Looking back, the Aldridges recall, "We depended on bomb-building for our survival and worked for peace as a hobby."

Eventually the Aldridge family decided that Bob should resign his job, even though it would be virtually impossible to find an engineering position in their area not tied to a military contract. Their style of living would have to be significantly altered. Yet, in seeking to pattern their lives according to the values of God's kingdom, the Aldridges increasingly found themselves led to a lifestyle of nonconformity to the world's values. In the eyes of the world, Bob's resignation from a secure and prestigious position was ridiculous, but from the perspective of the kingdom, it seemed right. Because of the change, the family consciously worked at simplifying their lives. In the process, they began to discover the "simple gifts" of faith and purposeful living. Janet and Bob write, "We are trying to be less greedy as we search for ways to reduce our own needs so there will be enough to go around. Life is still scary, but we attempt to follow our consciences and rely on faith."[9]

A Creative Anxiety

The Aldridges' decision did not eliminate all anxiety from their lives, but it did radically alter the nature of their anxiety. Perhaps Lloyd Ogilvie captures this movement best when he asserts,

> Jesus' cure for anxiety is anxiety. Is this a clever play on words? I think not. He suggests a creative anxiety which alone can burn out the smoldering fires of neurotic anxiety. His dynamic sweep of truth moves from the false causes of anxiety to the introduction of the reason for creative anxiety, and then to the practical word on where to begin.[10]

Creative anxiety– seeking first God's kingdom, grappling with issues related to simplicity and nonconformity and obedient discipleship, putting lesser things in perspective in order to experience "the need of only one thing" (Luke 10:42), discovering purpose and joy through commitment of one's life to Christ and Christ's lifestyle of compassion and grace, mercy, and peace– this is our calling. This is our challenge.

Responding to the Scriptures

1. The things for which I am most grateful to God are...

2. The specific ways I offer myself as a living sacrifice are...

3. That offering causes me to be at odds with the worldly standards of . . .

4. The worldly standards that present the greatest challenge to my faith are . . .

5. The circumstances that most cause my heart to sing are . . .

6. Acquaintances might describe my discipleship as radical in the areas of . . .

7. I would like to simplify my life by . . .

   and to achieve that I must . . .

8. Barriers to my seeking God's kingdom first are . . .

9. If I were explaining to a new believer the rewards of seeking God's kingdom first, I would say . . .

10. (To be completed following discussion) My learnings from this session are . . .

Preparation for the Next Session

1. Pray daily for yourself and the other participants.

2. Continue with your planned action responses.

3. Read and consider the scripture text and content in Chapter 7.

4. Complete REFLECTING ON THE SCRIPTURES and RESPONDING TO THE SCRIPTURES in Chapter 7.

7

A Faith That Works

Purpose

- To underscore the importance of living out our discipleship in deeds of mercy, justice, and peace

Reading the Scriptures

Read James 2:14-26.
My first responses to this passage are . . .

Exploring the Scriptures

While the letter of James has been one of the lesser-used books in the Scriptures, it is in fact

> one of the most exciting parts of the New Testament. It has a hard-hitting punch and a reality-oriented attitude that catch readers unaware and astound them, while also offering them practical guidelines for life . . .

James is an example of how the early church used and applied the words of Jesus to their daily life.[1]

The writing of James is very close to the teaching of Jesus, especially our Lord's Sermon on the Mount. And yet, at first glance, it may seem surprising that the author, likely the brother of Jesus who later became leader of the Jerusalem church, does not directly quote Jesus. But in the early church, before the Gospels were produced, the teachings of Jesus no doubt were communicated orally. Early Christians memorized Christ's teachings much as the Jewish faithful memorized those of their teachers. Because of this familiarity, the readers of the letter of James would readily recognize that James was reminding them of the teachings of Jesus. Indeed, it is quite possible that most of the proverbs and short sayings in James came from Jesus.[2]

One of the most hard-hitting sections of James' epistle is found in James 2:14-26. James cautions against a faith that does not go beyond intellectual agreement, a faith that does not affect one's whole being. James urges his fellow Christians instead to put on a faith that leads to action, for "faith divorced from deeds is lifeless as a corpse" (v. 26 NEB). The most familiar translation reads, "faith without works is dead" (KJV).

Yet there is a problem with this passage, for when James asserts that God's people are "justified by works and not by faith alone" (v. 24), he appears to contradict the influential teachings of the Apostle Paul. Paul's central theological conviction is that we are "justified by faith apart from works prescribed by the law" (Rom. 3:28). Paul is certain that we experience right relationship with God, not through our own efforts, but because of God's saving activity in Jesus Christ. To the Ephesians Paul writes, "For by grace you have been saved through faith, and this is not your own doing; it is the gift of God" (Eph. 2:8). Reformation leader Martin Luther found this apparent conflict between the writings of James and Paul so distressing that he spoke of the letter of James as "an epistle full of straw."

Luther even claimed that James "does violence to Scripture, and so contradicts Paul and all Scripture . . . I therefore refuse him a place among the writers of the true canon of my Bible."[3]

In contrast to Luther, many Christians today appreciate the letter of James, perhaps most because of its apparent reliance upon the Sermon on the Mount and its emphasis on discipleship. But what are we to make of James' declaration that we are justified in God's sight by our works? Is there any way of reconciling that declaration with Paul's powerful affirmation that salvation cannot be earned by human striving, but only received as a gracious gift from God?

A careful study of James makes it clear that the writer uses the word *faith* in two varying ways. One meaning is found chiefly in chapters 1 and 5 and may be roughly translated as "commitment" or "trust." When, for example, James speaks of "the prayer of faith" (5:15) as an integral part of the anointing for healing, he is referring to prayers offered in trust to God. That use of the word *faith* demonstrates an understanding of faith reasonably close to Paul's, who sees faith as a matter of believing with all our heart, all our being, that God through Christ brings us salvation and wholeness. The second view of faith James provides is found in 2:14-26. In that passage, faith signifies mere intellectual belief; it includes neither personal investment nor vital commitment.[4] It is this second view of faith that James criticizes. He is utterly convinced that our faith gives us resources for creative ministry and service in Christ's name. As a result, he is appalled whenever he encounters "faith" that does not lead to compassionate action, that does not make a significant difference in the faithful's lifestyle and relationships. To illustrate his point, James offers an example that could have happened in the fledgling Jerusalem church. He writes,

> If a brother or sister is naked and lacks daily food, and one of you says to them, "Go in peace; keep warm and eat your fill," and yet

you do not supply their bodily needs, what is the good of that? (2:15-16)

The answer is clear, is it not? It profits nothing. "So faith by itself, if it has no works, is dead" (v. 17). For James, the Christian faith must be a working faith, a faith that results in obedience to the teachings and Spirit of Christ. Discipleship is not an "extra" in the Christian life, something that can be added or subtracted at the individual's whim. Rather, it is central to the Christian life– a conviction Paul would surely share with James. In his familiar love chapter, you will recall, Paul cries out, "If I have all faith, so as to remove mountains, but do not have love, I am nothing" (1 Cor. 13:2). And to the Galatians Paul writes, "For in Christ Jesus neither circumcision nor uncircumcision counts for anything; the only thing that counts is *faith working through love"* (Gal. 5:6, italics added).

Perhaps James' message is most clearly stated in 2:22. Affirming Abraham as one who allowed his faith to inform and give shape to his actions, James continues, "You see that faith was active along with his works, and faith was brought to completion by the works." It is in this sense that James asks, "Was not our ancestor Abraham justified by works?" (v. 21). James sees a mutuality between faith and works. "Faith informs and motivates action; action matures faith. James is not rejecting one for the other but is instead insisting that the two are totally inseparable."[5]

Turning to Rahab as another model (v. 25), James reiterates this conviction that faith and works are inseparable. Rahab confesses faith in the God of the Israelites, and it is that faith that motivates her to risk her life, welcoming the Israelite spies and then helping them escape (see Josh. 2:1-21). Because Rahab's faith touched her whole being, leading to committed action, she is received by God as friend. Would not the Apostle Paul, convinced that we are justified by faith, celebrate Rahab's faith leading to action? Do not both Paul and James recognize and affirm that faith compels us to active discipleship? As one commentator concludes,

Actually the gap between Paul and James is much smaller than a superficial comparison of their words would suggest. Paul insists that justification is by faith, not by works, though he clearly expects faith to bear fruit in love. James cries down faith without deeds, but makes it clear that the faith he cries down is a barren intellectual assent not a vital commitment of the whole personality to God in Christ. It is this living and obedient trust that carries with it the promises made so often in the Bible to "them that believe."[6]

Reflecting on the Scriptures

1. How do you understand the relationship between faith and works?

2. Is James suggesting a return to salvation by way of the law, the same law against which Paul spoke?

3. What other passages of scripture does this passage bring to mind?

Applying the Scriptures

A Noble Calling

John Naas was on a preaching mission when he was seized by recruiting agents for the King of Prussia, Frederick William I, who ruled from 1713 to 1740. These were days when it was illegal to belong to any faith other than the ruler's chosen faith. Naas had chosen to follow Christ as one of an illegal church, the Brethren, Christians committed to Christ's call to nonresistance and peacemaking. The king had sent agents out all over Europe, to secure recruits, by fair means or foul, for his personal guard. All soldiers in that personal guard stood over six feet tall, and John Naas caught the eye of the recruiters because of his height.

When Naas refused to enlist voluntarily, he was tortured. His captors even hung him by his left thumb and the large toe of his right foot and threatened to leave John Naas in that painful and humiliating position until he submitted. Finally, fearing Naas might die, the agents cut him down and dragged him before Frederick William I, asking the king what they might do to convince Naas to enlist.

The king inquired of the Brethren leader why he would not participate in the personal guard. Replied John Naas, "I have already long ago enlisted into one of the noblest and best of enrollments and I would not, and could not, become a traitor to him." Surprised, the king asked for the identity of this competing king. "My captain," asserted Naas, "is the great Prince Emmanuel, our Lord, Jesus Christ. I have espoused his cause, and therefore, cannot and will not forsake him." The story has it that the king was so moved by John Naas' straightforward reply that he released Naas, giving him a gold coin.[7]

John Naas knew that faith without works is dead. The Christian faith, by definition, is a working faith, a faith that manifests itself in loyalty to Jesus Christ and obedience to Christ's teachings. The early Brethren leader chose not to rest, content with halfhearted commitment. Instead, he embraced a noble yet risky calling, allowing his faith in Christ Jesus to inform and motivate his actions, his very lifestyle.

The Real Thing

In like manner, are we not challenged yet today to live out our discipleship in deeds of justice and mercy, compassion and peace? Yet have we not all too often found ourselves similar to the one in James' example who failed to offer significant assistance to the brother or sister in need? Could it be that we have been fearful of embracing wholeheartedly a faith that expresses itself in creative discipleship?

The advertising world points to an elusive kind of happiness. Always happiness is one more purchase, one more product away. But life in Christ promises the real thing—lasting purpose and joy that comes as we commit our whole selves to God, seeking God's direction as we serve God's people.

Let Justice Roll Down

In his book *Let Justice Roll Down*, John Perkins tells his story of a faith that could not be satisfied with anything less than obedient discipleship. Perkins had grown up in Mississippi, but after the experience of having his brother die in his arms, brutally shot by a deputy in an unprovoked racial incident, Perkins left the state, vowing never to return. Yet after a conversion experience, Perkins felt God's call to return to Mississippi. Although they had developed a comfortable life elsewhere, Perkins and his family returned to establish a new congregation among his black brothers and sisters. At the same time, they developed a host of ministries aimed at economic justice and development as well as reconciliation and discipleship. Senator Mark Hatfield writes in the foreword to John Perkins' book:

The story of John Perkins reveals the transforming and revolutionary power of Jesus Christ.... It is a gripping portrayal of what happens when faith in Christ thrusts a person into the midst of the struggle against racism, oppression and injustice. It is about the costs of such discipleship– the jailings, the floggings, the despair, the sacrifice. And it is about the relentless hope and the limitless love which can be born in the hearts of those who follow Christ.[8]

Such is the nature of a faith that works. Relentless hope and limitless love flow from our hearts as we commit ourselves, heart and soul, to Jesus Christ.

Responding to the Scriptures

1. My faith is infused with vitality when...

2. My faith seems lifeless when...

3. Some areas of my faith that may still be at the intellectual stage of development are...

4. I can move them to the action level by...

5. "Good works" I have done that have been motivated by a sense of obligation have resulted in . . .

6. "Good works" I have done that have been motivated by love for Christ have resulted in . . .

7. The action that most matured my faith has been . . .

8. To someone new to Christianity, I would explain the need for "costly faith" and total commitment by . . .

9. My evaluation of where I am on the journey toward total commitment is . . .

10. (To be completed following discussion) My learnings from this session are . . .

Preparation for the Next Session

1. Pray daily for yourself and the other participants.

2. Continue with your planned action responses.

3. Read and consider the scripture text and content in Chapter 8.

4. Complete REFLECTING ON THE SCRIPTURES and RESPONDING TO THE SCRIPTURES in Chapter 8.

5. Begin to complete RESPONDING TO THE CALL FOR ACTION (found on page 90).

8

More Than Conquerors!

Purpose

- To celebrate the disciple's ultimate triumph amid the struggle and affliction of this world

Reading the Scriptures

Read Romans 8:31-39.
My first responses to this passage are...

Exploring the Scriptures

The eighth chapter of Romans surely ranks as one of the most powerful chapters in the Scriptures. As the Apostle Paul writes to the Christians at Rome, he is setting forth his understanding of the gospel of Jesus Christ, "the power of God for salvation to everyone who has faith" (1:16). At the heart of Paul's faith is the conviction that we are made right with God, not through our own action, but as a result of God's initiative in Christ. After examining humankind's need for redemption (1:18– 3:30) and asserting that Christ Jesus opens the way for us to experience salvation (3:21–4:25), Paul highlights, beginning in chapter five, what it means for us to be justified in God's sight, to experience new life in Christ. The Apostle's affirmation of Christ Jesus as the source of our hope and life reaches its climax in chapter eight. Chapter 8 "furnishes a wealth of ways of describing the Christian life"[1] – a life of freedom from the law of sin and death (vv. 1-2); a walk according to the Spirit rather than the flesh (vv. 3-4); a mind centered on the things of the Spirit, that which pleases God (vv. 5-8); being fully alive through the Spirit of God and the gift of Christ in us (vv. 9-11); being children and heirs of God, along with Christ Jesus (vv. 12-17); a life that shares Christ's sufferings (v. 18); a life of eager longing and hope (vv. 19-25); a life of prayer (vv. 26-27); and a life of assurance, knowing that God is working for good with all who love God and who are called by God (vv. 28-30).

The culmination comes in 8:31-39, as Paul confidently assures his fellow Christians that "we are more than conquerors" through him [Christ] who loved us (v. 37). "Overwhelming victory is ours" through Christ, the Revised English Bible reads. That assurance is based upon all that Paul has written thus far in the epistle. "With all this in mind," Paul questions, "what are we to say! If God is on our side, who is against us?" (v. 31 REB). C. K. Barrett reminds us that Paul's question is not whether we are on God's side, but whether God is on ours.[2] If God is– and Paul clearly is convinced of that fact– then we may face all manner of danger and difficulty, but no one can alter the good news that God redeems us and makes us whole.

Paul pictures in these verses a court of law. God, who is the judge, is also the advocate appearing for us.[3] No opponent, nothing standing against us, can possibly triumph over God. The visible proof that there is no power greater than the power of God is God's gift of Jesus Christ. God "did not withhold his own Son but gave him up for all of us" (v. 32). What Paul says of God, God said of Abraham when Abraham demonstrated utter loyalty by being willing to sacrifice his son Isaac at God's command (Gen. 22:16). It is as if Paul is saying, "Think of the greatest human example in the world of a [person's] loyalty to God; God's loyalty to you is like that."[4] Given such self-giving love, "how can [God] fail to lavish every other gift upon us?" (v. 32 REB).

To emphasize the extravagant love of God, Paul speaks once again in verses 33-34 of the God who justifies bringing us into right relationship with him. The construction of these verses is somewhat unclear, but the message is apparent. People of faith are "God's elect" (v. 33). No one has a right to condemn, except the judge of all people, Jesus Christ. Yet far from condemning, Christ sits at God's right hand, the seat of honor, interceding for us and assuring our ultimate security. The Revised English Bible translation provides clarity:

> Who will bring a charge against those whom God has chosen? Not God, who acquits! Who will pronounce judgment? Not Christ, who died, or rather rose again; not Christ, who is at God's right hand and pleads our cause! (vv. 33-34)

Paul continues his series of rhetorical questions with "a poet's fervor and a lover's rapture" as he sings of how nothing can separate us from the love of God in our Risen Lord.[5] "Then what can separate us from the love of Christ? Can affliction or hardship? Can persecution, hunger, nakedness, danger, or sword?" (v. 35 REB). The Apostle, no doubt, is thinking autobiographically here, recalling that he has personally encountered– and overcome, with Christ's help– many of the dangers cited (see 2 Cor. 11:23-28). Paul also recognizes that all followers of Jesus may well encounter hostile opposition, for the message of Christ so frequently is at odds with the prevailing values and morés of the world. Paul has this in mind when quoting in verse 36 from Psalm 44:22, "For your sake we are being killed all day long; we are accounted as sheep to be slaughtered." Just as Jesus' death occurred in accordance with the Scriptures, so also the sufferings of Christians. "God does not remove such trials from our path; they are overcome in an *overwhelming victory.*"[6] Rather than dividing us from Christ, difficulties may well draw us closer to Christ. They remind us that we need to rely upon Christ, that we cannot go it alone in life.

It is Paul's inner certainty of that "overwhelming victory" that leads to the ringing conclusion of verses 37 through 39:

> In all these things we are more than conquerors through him who loved us. For I am convinced that neither death, nor life, nor angels, nor rulers, nor things present, nor things to come, nor powers, nor height, nor depth, nor anything else in all creation, will be able to separate us from the love of God in Christ Jesus our Lord.

It's a glorious affirmation of the Lordship of Jesus Christ. Nothing can separate us from Christ the Lord, not even death. As Paul cries out to the Philippians, "For to me, living is Christ, and dying is gain" (1:21).

Competing spiritual powers, too, cannot separate us from Christ's love. The people of Paul's day were certain that the world was controlled by evil spirits and superhuman powers.[7] These powers, as well as the planets and stars under which they were born, determined peoples' destiny. "Height" was the time when a star was at its zenith and its influence the greatest; "depth" was the moment when a star was at its lowest, waiting to rise and gain influence over the lives of people. In effect Paul is reminding the Christians at Rome that even the spirits and the stars are powerless to separate them from God's wondrous love. Indeed, no matter what terrifying thing this world or any other world can produce, it cannot separate them from God.[8] In Christ we are more than conquerors. We experience victory even amid life's struggles and afflictions.

Reflecting on the Scriptures

1. What makes the giving of one's only son so significant?

2. What possibility does this scripture give to God's condemning those for whom his son has died?

3. If nothing separates us from the love of God, why do so many people stand alienated from God?

4. What other passages of scripture does this passage bring to mind?

Applying the Scriptures

A Joyful Confidence

Mennonite pastor John Drescher relates the story of a missionary traveling on the same plane as a group of American soldiers. The soldiers had just completed a tour of duty in the Korean War and were celebrating their travel home. Other passengers were drawn into the festivity, and on several occasions the missionary was asked if she would like a drink or a cigarette. Each time she answered kindly, "No, thank you, I don't need it."

Her response intrigued several of the soldiers, and finally they asked her, "Would you tell us why you keep saying that?"

The woman responded, "I would be glad to. When you take a drink of liquor, an alcoholic beverage, or a cigarette, you do it because you are seeking joy. It's supposed to bring joy and satisfaction. Isn't that right?"

When they agreed, she continued. "Well, you see, I already have joy inside. I don't need the drink or the cigarette."

"Where did you find this joy?"

"At the end of my rope. I found Jesus the Giver of real joy at the end of my rope," she answered.[9]

The Apostle Paul, too, found Jesus, the Giver of real joy and satisfaction, of lasting purpose and hope. More accurately, Jesus found Paul, and in the process he transformed and redirected Paul's life. Whereas earlier as Saul, he breathed fire and vengeance upon the early Christians, now as the Apostle Paul, he began to breathe a joyful confidence in God and to share God's gracious love with others. God became more than an abstraction; God became for Paul a living reality, one worthy of trust and confidence.

The Gospel "Down in Our Guts"

Baptist pastor John Claypool speaks of a transforming encounter with God through Jesus Christ as experiencing the gospel "down in our guts."[10] That is to say, life in Christ is a matter of discovering– in the very core of our being– that we need not earn God's love. Rather, we receive God's love as a gift. We experience grace, knowing deep within us that "God is for us" and that nothing in all creation can cut us loose from the goodness and grace of God.

When that good news infuses us, heart and soul, we become more than conquerors. We learn to pray with Ruth Harms Calkin,

> God, I may fall flat on my face; I may fail until I feel old and beaten and done in. Yet your love for me is changeless. All the music may go out of my life, my private world may shatter to dust. Even so, you will hold me in the palm of your steady hand. . . . Nothing can separate me from your measureless love– pain can't, disappointment can't, anguish can't. Yesterday, today, tomorrow can't. The loss of my dearest love can't. Death can't. Life can't. Riots, war, insanity, unidentity, hunger, neurosis, disease– none of these things nor all of them heaped together can budge the fact that I am dearly loved, completely forgiven, and forever free through Jesus Christ your beloved Son.[11]

A Place to Stand

Who but God could conceive a love that knows no limits, that cannot be broken by difficulty and affliction, that will not let go? We can do no other but receive that love as gift and respond in grateful discipleship.

Several centuries before Christ, the Greek mathematician and inventor Archimedes asserted, "Give me a place to stand and I will move the earth."[12] When we experience the gospel "down in our guts," when we live in the joyful confidence of God's love, we discover that place to stand. We find something– we find Someone– on whom to stake our lives. In Christ we find not only a place to stand, but a place to live and to serve. Christ Jesus makes us "more than conquerors," empowering us to live and proclaim good news whether we face plenty or hunger, abundance or want, comfort or affliction.

In all these things we are more than conquerors through him who loved us. For I am convinced that neither death, nor life, nor angels, nor rulers, nor things present, nor things to come, nor powers, nor height, nor depth, nor anything else in all creation, will be able to separate us from the love of God in Christ Jesus our Lord. (Rom. 8:37-39)

Responding to the Scriptures

1. I have felt victorious in my life when ...

2. I have experienced the Spirit working to bring me into right relationship with God when ...

3. I am most confident of my ultimate security when ...

4. I have felt separated from God's love when ...

5. Difficulties that have drawn me closer to Christ are ...

6. I have sometimes sought joy and satisfaction outside God's kingdom by . . .

7. My greatest faith triumph has been . . .

8. I can help new believers discover that they are "more than conquerors" by . . .

9. (To be completed following discussion) My learnings from this session are . . .

Responding to the Call for Action

1. The new things I have learned that are calling me to grow in Christian discipleship are...

2. The actions to which they are calling me are...

3. The new things I have learned that are calling me to help disciple others are...

4. The actions to which they are calling me are...

5. During the next four weeks, I will seek to grow in Christian discipleship and disciple others by...

   I will ask _____ to help me be accountable for the above actions.

Endnotes

Introduction

1. Philip Teng, "Twelve Crises in the Apostolic Church," *Chinese Churches Today* (March, 1979), p. 38.

Chapter 1. God and God Alone

1. J. Coert Rylaardsdam, "The Book of Exodus: Introduction," in *The Interpreter's Bible*, vol. 1 (Nashville: Abingdon Press, 1952), p. 846.
2. Ibid., p. 833.
3. B. Davie Napier, "The Book of Exodus," in *The Layman's Bible Commentary*, vol. 3 (Richmond, Va.: John Knox Press, 1963), p. 77.
4. Ibid., p. 78.
5. J. Edgar Park, "The Book of Exodus: Exposition," in *The Interpreter's Bible*, vol. 1 (Nashville: Abingdon Press, 1952), p. 980.
6. Joy Davidman, *Smoke on the Mountain: An Interpretation of the Ten Commandments* (Philadelphia: The Westminster Press, 1954), pp. 23-24.
7. Clarence Jordan, *Sermon on the Mount* (Valley Forge, Pa.: Judson Press, 1952), p. 93.
8. Henri J. M. Nouwen, *The Living Reminder* (New York: The Seabury Press, 1977), pp. 30-31.
9. Dietrich Bonhoeffer, *The Cost of Discipleship* (New York: Macmillan Publishing Co., Inc., 1963), p. 41.

Chapter 2. The Importance of the Word

1. William Barclay, *The Letters to Timothy, Titus and Philemon* (Philadelphia: The Westminster Press, 1975), p. 13.
2. Holmes Rolston, "Thessalonians, Timothy, Titus, Philemon," in *The Layman's Bible Commentary*, vol. 23 (Richmond, Va.: John Knox Press, 1963), p. 109.
3. Vernon Grounds, *Radical Commitment: Getting Serious About Christian Growth* (Portland, Ore.: Multnomah Press, 1984), p. 51.
4. Ibid., p. 16.
5. Walter Brueggemann, *The Bible Makes Sense* (Atlanta: John Knox Press, 1983), p. 17.

6. *Ein Geringer Schein,* pp. 1-2, translated by and quoted in Vernard Eller, *Kierkegaard and Radical Discipleship* (Princeton, New Jersey: Princeton University Press, 1968), pp. 419-420.
7. Anna B. Mow, *Say "Yes" to Life!* (Grand Rapids, Mich.: Zondervan Publishing House, 1961), p. 132.
8. Tom Sine, *The Mustard Seed Conspiracy* (Waco, Texas: Word Books, 1981), p. 119.

Chapter 3. When You Pray

1. Jordan, p. 15.
2. Lloyd John Ogilvie, *A Life Full of Surprises* (Nashville: Abingdon Press, 1969), p. 101.
3. Ibid., p. 105.
4. Earl F. Palmer, *The Enormous Exception: Meeting Christ in the Sermon on the Mount* (Waco, Texas: Word Books, 1986), p. 66.
5. Jordan, p. 84.
6. Palmer, p. 66.
7. Archibald M. Hunter, *A Pattern for Life: An Exposition of the Sermon on the Mount* (Philadelphia: The Westminster Press, 1965), p. 71.
8. Maxie Dunnam, *The Workbook of Living Prayer* (Nashville: The Upper Room, 1974), p. 51.
9. Hunter, p. 73.
10. Dunnam, p. 58.
11. Jordan, p. 89.
12. Dunnam, p. 12.
13. Mow, p. 149.
14. Dunnam, p. 114.
15. Douglas V. Steere, *Dimensions of Prayer* (New York: Harper and Row, 1963), pp. 24-25.

Chapter 4. Praise to the Lord

1. Bernhard W. Anderson, *Out of the Depths: The Psalms Speak for Us Today* (Philadelphia: The Westminster Press, 1970), p. 3.
2. Ibid., p. 80.
3. William R. Taylor, "The Book of Psalms: Exegesis, Psalm 100," in *The Interpreter's Bible,* vol. 4 (Nashville: Abingdon Press, 1955), p. 532.
4. Ibid., pp. 532-533.
5. Ibid., p. 534.
6. Anderson, pp. 110-111.
7. John Killinger, *The Cup and the Waterfall: The Adventure of Living in the Present Moment* (New York: Paulist Press, 1983), pp. 1-2.
8. Robert E. Webber, *Worship Is a Verb* (Waco, Texas: Word Books, 1985), p. 31.

9. John M. Drescher, *Spirit Fruit* (Scottdale, Pennsylvania: Herald Press, 1974), p. 86.
10. Ibid., p. 99.
11. Dunnam, p. 70.
12. James F. White, *New Forms of Worship* (Nashville: Abingdon Press, 1971), p. 42.

Chapter 5. Walking by the Spirit.

1. Archibald M. Hunter, *The Letters of Paul to the Galatians, Ephesians, Philippians, Colossians*, in The Layman's Bible Commentary Series, vol. 22 (Richmond, Va.: John Knox Press, 1959), p. 7.
2. William Barclay, *The Letters to the Galatians and Ephesians* (Philadelphia: The Westminister Press, 1976), p. 44.
3. William Neil, *The Letter of Paul to the Galatians*, in The Cambridge Bible Commentary (Cambridge, England: Cambridge University Press, 1967), p. 79.
4. Hunter, *Letters*, p. 38.
5. Ibid.
6. Neil, p. 82.
7. Ibid.
8. Elizabeth O'Connor, *Our Many Selves* (New York: Harper and Row, 1971), p. 3.
9. Henri Nouwen quoted in *Ministry and Solitude* by James C. Fenhagen (New York: The Seabury Press, 1981), pp. 80-81.

Chapter 6. 'Tis a Gift to Be Simple

1. Kenneth J. Foreman, *Romans, 1 and 2 Corinthians*, in The Layman's Bible Commentary, vol. 21 (Richmond, Va.: John Knox Press, 1961), p. 50.
2. Ernest Best, *The Letter of Paul to the Romans*, in The Cambridge Bible Commentary (Cambridge, England: Cambridge University Press, 1967), p. 138.
3. Foreman, p. 53.
4. Ogilvie, p. 112.
5. John W. Miller, *The Christian Way: A Guide to the Christian Life Based on the Sermon on the Mount* (Scottdale, Pennsylvania: Herald Press, 1969), pp. 80-81.
6. Ogilvie, pp. 112-113.
7. E. Stanley Jones, *The Unshakable Kingdom and the Unchanging Person* (Nashville: Abingdon Press, 1972), p. 54.
8. "Simple Gifts," in *The Brethren Songbook* (Elgin, Ill.: The Brethren Press, 1974), hymn 23.

9. Janet and Bob Aldridge, "Therefore Choose Life," *Sojourners*, vol. 6, no. 2 (February, 1977), pp. 29-31.
10. Ogilvie, p. 111.

Chapter 7. A Faith That Works

1. Peter H. Davids, *James*, in *A Good News Commentary* series (New York: Harper and Row Publishers, 1983), p. xv.
2. Ibid., pp. xxxii-xxxiii.
3. William Barclay, *The Letters of James and Peter* (Philadelphia: The Westminster Press, 1976), pp. 6-8.
4. Davids, p. xxx.
5. Ibid., p. 42.
6. R. R. Williams, *The Letters of John and James* (Cambridge, England: Cambridge University Press, 1965), p. 117.
7. Donald Durnbaugh, "The Lesson in History," *Brethren Adult Quarterly*, vol. 73, no. 2 (April-June, 1958), p. 57.
8. John Perkins, *Let Justice Roll Down* (Glendale, Calif.:Regal Books, 1976), p. 7.

Chapter 8. More Than Conquerors!

1. Foreman, p. 42.
2. C. K. Barrett, *A Commentary on the Epistle to the Romans* (New York: Harper and Row, Publishers, 1957), p. 172.
3. Best, pp. 102-103.
4. William Barclay, *The Letter to the Romans* (Philadelphia: The Westminster Press, 1975), pp. 115-116.
5. Ibid., p. 117.
6. Best, p. 103.
7. Ibid., p. 104.
8. Barclay, pp. 118-119.
9. Drescher, p. 88.
10. John R. Claypool, *The Preaching Event* (Waco, Texas: Word Books, 1980), p. 76.
11. Ray C. Stedman, *From Guilt to Glory*, vol. 1 (Waco, Texas: Word Books, 1978), p. 259.
12. Elton Trueblood, *A Place to Stand* (New York: Harper and Row Publishers, 1969), p. 13.

WITHDRAWN
from
Funderburg Library